San Juan Islands...and Beyond

– A Photographer's Journey –

Photography by Karyn F. King

"Every photograph has a story and some are a life lesson." —Karyn F. King

PASSION. CREATION. INSPIRATION.™

San Juan Islands...and Beyond

– A Photographer's Journey –

Photography by Karyn F. King

Karyn King is a freelance photographer who has spent many years capturing the beauty of the Pacific Northwest. She's also the proprietor of PhotosHappen.com and SanJuanIslandsPhotographer.com, producing a yearly calendar note cards and framed prints. Her work can be seen in stores and galleries throughout the San Juan Islands and Seattle. Most of the proceeds from sales are donated to local community outreach programs such as The Whale Museum, ASPCA, WWF, and local community and animal outreach programs.

First Edition

Layout and map art by Anita Jones (Another Jones Graphics)

Printed in Korea

ISBN: 978-0-615-56038-0

$\mathcal{T}$ake a journey with me through the San Juan Islands and beyond as I share some magical moments, images and thoughts. With more than 50,000 images of the northwest, it was not easy to choose which I felt best represented the islands, wildlife and landscapes with their ever changing beauty.

The first section is devoted to images of orcas, or killer whales. They are one of the most fascinating wildlife icons seen in the San Juan Islands, they are playful, intelligent and social animals. They make unique calls to communicate with each other and use echolocation to find food.

Usually we see the Southern Resident Killer Whale (SRKW) pods or the transient pods. The orcas that are seen in our local waters are part of the Southern Resident Community, composed of J, K and L pods. They feed mainly on salmon and use sound to find fish, while transient killer whales have developed quiet hunting techniques to successfully catch their marine mammal prey. Seeing them, being in their presence, there was a palpable feeling of connection with these enormous elegant beings as if we were part of their family.

Orcas can be seen all year in the San Juan Islands but regularly May through September, however, the whales aren't on a schedule. You never know when or where they may show up. In 2005 they were placed on the endangered species list.

I continue to be in awe of the natural beauty of the Northwest and excited to be able to share my "view of the world." Come along on my five year photographic journey by air, sea and land as I explore the living beauty of the San Juan Islands and surrounding area.

Orcas

Orca breach in Haro Strait.

Glistening in the sunshine, an orca rejoices in Haro Strait near Lime Kiln Park on San Juan Island.

Magnificent killer whale!

Baby orca spyhops in the security of its mother's presence.

Whales "blow" is the term used to describe the mist that arises from an exhale as the whale comes to the surface to breathe.

Spyhopping and breaching are other remarkable activities which allow the orca to become familiar with its surroundings.

7

Found in every ocean of the world the killer whales are listed as endangered species.

Moments apart, from
start of a breach (right) to
completion (far right) this
was taken near shore
at Stuart Island.

Sailboat surprise, some say the breaching and jumping seems like an expression of joyfulness.

Orca breach.

An orca spyhops at Turn Point Lighthouse on Stuart Island.

Oblivious, people look toward shore as this orca quietly spyhops beside their small boat.

Cruisin'

Wildlife

Popeye, the resident seal hanging out near the fish market in the Friday Harbor marina.

Popeye makes a splash.

The perfect pair, the colorful mallard male is called a drake, the female a hen.

Rarely seen in the San Juan Islands, the Horned Puffin stands out

Colorful Eider also rarely seen in the San Juan Islands.

National bird symbol of the United States, bald eagles are believed to mate for life, building one of the world's largest nests.

Bald eagles get their distinctive white markings when they become adults at 4-5 years.

The mature bald eagle is an easily recognizable and impressive bird. Females are usually larger than males, weighing 10-14 pounds with a 6 ½-7 foot wingspan. Males usually weigh 8-10 pounds with a 6-6½ foot wingspan.

Not all animal species are native to the island. Resident non-native Red Fox and Grey (Gray) Fox seen on San Juan Island.

Autumn colors reflect in local waters.

Island Sunsets

Sunset over Rosario Strait gives the impression of pastels on canvas.

Lopez Island looks on as the sun's evening rays light up Rosario Strait.

Heading home before dark, another impressive sunset in the San Juan Islands.

Right place, right time. A bald eagle cruises home to Washington Park on Fidalgo Island.

Magnificent mammatus clouds float above Lopez Island at dusk.

The ever changing colors of sunset in Rosario Strait after sunset.

Nature's artwork, an aerial view of the San Juan Islands at sundown.

Sunset on the rocks, South Beach, San Juan Island

Sunset at Fisherman Bay, Lopez Island.

Marina and Bay Views

Ahhh...

One ray of light foretells the calm before the storm.

Upside down reflection at Friday Harbor Marina

Picture-perfect island morning . . . when it's hard to tell which way is up and which way is down

Peek-a-boo view of an idyllic Echo Bay while hiking on Sucia Island.

Cattle Point Lighthouse sits atop this windswept bluff on San Juan Island and overlooks the Strait of Juan de Fuca. Livestock were unloaded here before the Pig War.

Lime Kiln State Park lighthouse rests on the rocky shore of San Juan Island.
This area is known as Whale Watch Park for its prime orca viewing.

Lime Kiln Lighthouse, the only other lighthouse on San Juan Island, once guided mariners through Dead Man's Bay. In 1985 the lighthouse and surrounding sea were dedicated as a whale sanctuary and research station for marine mammal scientists.

Colorful kayaks await those who want to see the shoreline and marine life up close and personal.

Orcas Island's Mount Constitution is the highest point in the San Juan Islands. At its summit stands a stone observation tower constructed by the Civilian Conservation Corps in 1936 to look like a medieval watchtower. It offers panoramic views of the surrounding islands, the Cascade Mountains and Sucia Island State Park.

As seen from Mount Constitution's observation tower, Sucia Island Marine State park.

Typical modes of transportation around the San Juan Islands are by ferry and float plane.

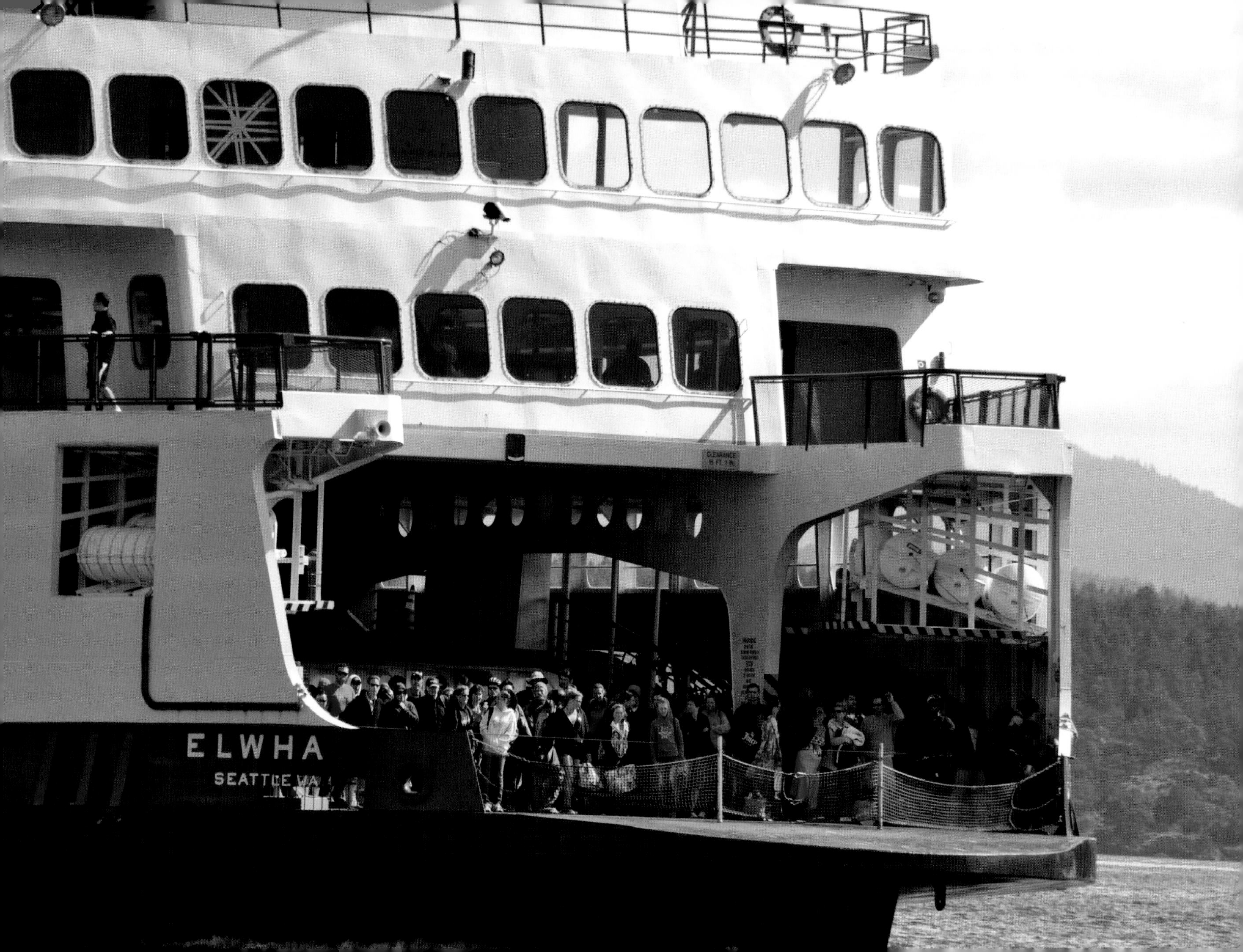
CLEARANCE
15 FT. 1 IN.
ELWHA

A ferry basks in the evening glow at Friday Harbor before heading toward Anacortes on Fidalgo Island.

The Elwha leaves Friday Harbor and the snow-capped Cascades on a crisp Spring day.

ries Elwha and Sealth light up the midnight-blue waters of Friday Harbor

A ferry travels the island waters at night like an ornament on the water.

Shaw Island is the smallest of the four San Juan Islands serviced by the Washington State Ferries.

Aerial Island Images

Tranquil setting of Fisherman Bay at Lopez Island, the marinas and Lopez Village are close by.

Washington State Ferries, the primary link to the mainland, transport people and their vehicles to and from the San Juan Islands

White sailboats dot the blue waters of Blind Bay, Shaw Island.

Northwest area of San Juan Island, a boat jets out from Mosquito Pass. Roche Harbor can be seen in the upper center.

Lime and cement mining put Roche Harbor on the 19th century map. Today, it's filled with natural beauty,

Aerial view of Friday Harbor.

Breathtaking view of the Sucia archipelago—Sucia Island Marine State Park has hiking trails, bays and coves for boaters, each unique and peaceful.

Other Points of Interest

Orcas Landing, where visitors come by ferry to see the many wonders Orcas Island has to offer.

The Madrona Grill and the historical McMillin dining room overlook Roche Harbor marina.

Our Lady of Good Voyage Chapel at Roche Harbor was constructed in the late 1880s and is an historical landmark.

Listed in the National Register of Historic Places, the Hotel de Haro at Roche Harbor still features many rooms appointed with original antiques.

Adorned in bright flowers, the Adieu Trellis leads the traveler along the cobblestone walkway to the Roche Harbor marina.

The Afterglow Vista Mausoleum was built by John S. McMillin to serve as the family tomb. The centerpiece is a large stone table surrounded by stone chairs. The family members were entombed in the chairs allowing them to "be gathered" around the table.

One of the many sculptures set against the impressive backdrop of the 19-acre Westcott Bay San Juan Island Museum and Sculpture Park. (*One Otter or the Other* bronze by Mike Hollern.)

San Juan Island National Historical Park, also known as American Camp (opposite page) and English Camp (above), is located on San Juan Island. U.S. and British forces set up camp here in 1859 in response to a border dispute triggered by the killing of a pig.

Rolling mounds of lavender fields in bloom can be seen as the summer season begins.

Fourth of July fireworks light up the sky and water
at Friday Harbor marina.

The 'Cutthroat Pirates' fly the Jolly Roger at Friday Harbor's Fourth of July parade. Fun and frivolity rule the day!

Tour de Lopez brings thousands of bicyclists in the late spring.

...and Beyond

Flying over the San Juan Islands I was inspired to see more of the area around Seattle. These next images are included to give a taste of some iconic images beyond the San Juan Islands. Deception Pass Bridge and State Park, Cap Sante Boat Haven, La Conner's Rainbow Bridge, Point Wilson Lighthouse, Mount Rainier, Seattle's waterfront, Seattle Center, Seattle's Space Needle, Hiram M. Chittenden Locks, Mount Shuksan, Butchart Gardens in the spring, Victoria, BC., and Tulips in the Skagit Valley.

An aerial view of Deception Pass State Park is the most visited state park in Washington with over two million visitors each year.

The placid waters of Cap Sante Boat Haven in Anacortes act as the sunset's looking glass.

LaConner's Rainbow Bridge, a Registered National Landmark connects Fidalgo Island to the mainland.

Point Wilson Lighthouse near Port Townsend, marks the west entrance to the Puget Sound. It is the turning point
from the Strait of Juan de Fuca into Admiralty Inlet.

Glorious Mount Rainier looms over Seattle as ferries treat passengers to a perfect day.

Seattle Rocks! Distinctive Experience Music Project (EMP) building stands out, the colorful lower right structure.

Seattle's Space Needle up close
and personal.

Seattle to Bellevue via the
Hiram M. Chittenden Locks.
The locks separate the fresh water
of Lake Washington from the salt
water of the Puget Sound.

North Cascades National Park, Mount Shuksan's first snow and last of the fall flowers.

Butchart Gardens in the spring, Victoria, BC.

Tulip rainbow in the Skagit Valley.

About the Author

My interest in photography began when I was eight years old, I still have my original Kodak Brownie camera to prove it! In my early twenties I exhibited my photographs, mostly seascapes as I was boating off the California coast.

Photography interrupted…
I went on to teach and earn a master's degree in oceanography. Then I pursued a technical career at NASA's Jet Propulsion Laboratory in Pasadena.

Since I moved to Washington in 1989, I have focused on the striking beauty of the Northwest and the San Juan Islands, my most awe-inspiring location to date. Although I've been photographing western Washington, Alaska and British Columbia for over twenty years, I find there are still endless possibilities to explore. Some favorite subjects are island sunsets, orca whales and wildlife, yachts in motion, Japanese gardens and most maritime activities.

Viewing life through my camera lens offers more than a change of perspective. It renews my soul, lifts my spirits and allows me to savor the wonders of nature long after I've returned home.

Photography has taught me many lessons, the most valuable of which is to let go of expectations so that all possibilities may unfold, especially the ones you can't imagine. After all, that's how *San Juan Islands and Beyond, A Photographer's Journey* was born.

You can find my calendars, note cards and prints at galleries and stores throughout Seattle and the San Juan Islands. More information and images can be found at SanJuanIslandsPhotographer.com and PhotosHappen.com.

A large portion of the proceeds from the sales are donated to local outreach programs and animal rescue organizations such as The Whale Museum, NOAH, ASPCA, Red Cross Disaster Relief, World Wildlife Fund, PCC Farmland Trust, Cascade Animal Shelter and other local animal shelters.

Acknowledgements: On this journey of exploration, I have received the support of many individuals. I'd like to acknowledge my rocket scientist husband, Dr. David King, who has been my cheerleader, my Captain (aargh!) and my lovely assistant throughout this process. And to Dr. Dieter Zube, my extraordinary pilot, whose skills, knowledge and expertise helped me "get" that aerial shot. There are several others I wish to acknowledge but they are too humble to allow me to mention their names, you know who you are!

Index of Images

Every photograph has a story and some are a life lesson. —Karyn F. King